I0159242

FINDING PURPOSE

By L. Leonard Taylor

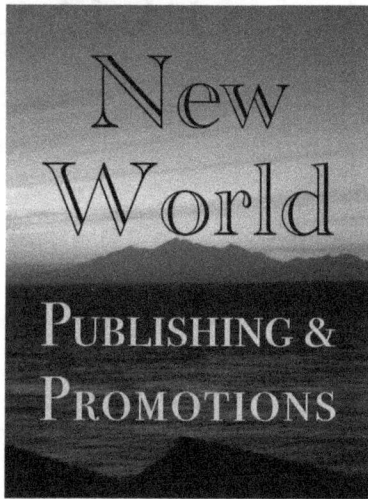

Published By

New
World

PUBLISHING &
PROMOTIONS

Lahaina, Hawaii, USA

Copyright © 2013
L. Leonard Taylor

All rights reserved. No parts of this book may be
reproduced in any form, except for the inclusion of
brief quotations in review, without the expressed
written permission of the author or publisher.

For Carl & Tarra Kalonzo, may their
union bear fruit of great purpose

"When you are inspired by some great purpose, some extraordinary project, all your thoughts break their bonds: Your mind transcends limitations, your consciousness expands in every direction, and you find yourself in a new, great and wonderful world. Dormant forces, faculties and talents become alive, and you discover yourself to be a greater person by far than you ever dreamed yourself to be."

~ Patanjali

TABLE OF CONTENTS

Preface

I wanted a different life. I didn't like my uniform. I didn't like my paycheck. I didn't like feeling my intelligence was unappreciated. I didn't like my job and my job was at the center of my life. What I wore to work and what I was paid defined me. My self esteem was intimately connected to my work clothes and my compensation. My unconscious purpose in life was to be prosperous and feel good about it by getting a job that required a tie and a fat paycheck. Ego fulfillment was a big part of my purpose. My passion to feel better about myself by wearing a suit and tie was the driving force, the energy that moved me. Months later, I got what I wanted, using six steps.

Twelve years after putting on a tie, I wanted to take it off. Job, income and status realized, I was not satisfied with my role in this dysfunctional world. Inequality, war, suffering, greed and I was part of the perpetual machine. What was my true purpose in this life? If my tie was so valuable, where was my peace, where was my happiness?

L. Leonard Taylor

"Finding Purpose" was an afterthought to writing "Six Steps to Living on Purpose". My first major transformation occurred without giving conscious thought to my purpose - it defaulted to what I craved - a suit and tie. Wanting to make another big change in life, I decided to revisit the steps previously taken. Yes, six very specific steps drove my transition and awarded me a life of my purpose - ego satisfaction - with prosperity, man's first and foremost priority. Now, with needs being met, what would I become? I needed purpose. I would write, but writing is a passion, so what would I write? I began a search for my personal purpose, because while my passion was writing I felt I was here to serve humanity in some way. How would I ever figure out what would be my purpose in life?

This little book, *Finding Purpose,* is an expanded chapter from my book, *Six Steps to Living on Purpose.* This book is broken into two parts and summarizes the easiest and most complete method to finding personal purpose in your life. Part I is a *Philosophy of Purpose* and the basis for Part II: *Finding Your Personal Purpose.* Part I and II are mutually exclusive, meaning you need not read both to find a purpose. Part I is an explanation of why purpose is critical to sustain our environment, perpetuate the human species and conscious human evolution. Part II will aid you in identifying your reason for being here - your purpose in life - by examining four intimate areas of your life and how they relate to each other and their potential impact on you, those around you and humanity.

The purpose finding tool in Part II will shed light on the most prudent course for achieving personal peace, highlight your path to rewarding prosperity, and show how your efforts can provide the most positive impact on humanity. This process clearly identifies your best methods, mediums, and tools for pursuing your purpose and where to find your most appealing missions of service to humanity. More importantly, your life's purpose will be revealed from your own knowledge of self, in relation to your community and the world. With your purpose in hand, you will be equipped to find a more fulfilling life and be prepared to follow *Six Steps to Living on Purpose*.

The six step method of implementing change is not dependent on any *particular* purpose, but rather on a *well defined* purpose. The six step process will, indeed, catapult you in the direction of your desires, allowing you to live your purpose, be it noble or treacherous. However, it would be irresponsible to provide anyone with such a life changing, humanity impacting, powerful tool without considering those who might unknowingly pursue a purpose capable of negatively impacting our world. With that in mind, if you have a preconceived purpose or if you haven't considered your life's effect on humanity, please consider the statement of warning on the next page as it is found in my book *Six Steps to Living on Purpose* - it was written specifically for you.

Warning: Using the six step transformational process requires a well-defined thought-through purpose, preferably a "Life Purpose." Implementation of something other than your clear life purpose, based in service, may lead to greed and ego based quests, resulting in a further separation of humankind. A purpose not grounded in service can lead to unhappiness, feelings of an unfulfilled life and may have disastrous effects on humanity. Please read the previous "How to Find Your Purpose" chapter to clearly identify your life's purpose before continuing with the next step in your transformational process.

L. Leonard Taylor

Part I

The Philosophy of Purpose

*There can be no greater loss to the world
than that of a prosperous human being
without a purpose that serves humanity.*

~ L. Leonard Taylor

The Foundation - Service as Humankind's Purpose

Six Steps to Living on Purpose does not require you to understand or have a philosophy for your purpose. In fact, this book is not one of the six steps at all. Indeed, you may bring your own purpose, dispense with this book or skip over to the actual process of finding your purpose in Part II of this book. This philosophical review of purpose is an examination of the basis and the reasons for finding and living a life based on a purpose of serving humanity.

There are two widely held beliefs surrounding man's purpose for living. Both beliefs require some leap of faith, as does any philosophy, and one is likely to resonate with you as the reason or purpose of man's existence. The first belief is commonly held by nearly all of the world's religions - *we are here to glorify our creator.* The second belief is widely held by science, secular based philosophies and those less likely to be aligned with religion or science and captures nearly all in the balance of human inhabitants on earth - *we are here for the survival of the species.*

In whichever category one places oneself, a common theme remains: Man's purpose in life is to maintain humanity and all life supporting our ecological balance. To maintain life is to serve life.

"Service is the rent you pay for your space on earth."
~ Shirley Chisholm

Mankind's Principles of Purpose

The diversity of human conditions, beliefs and cultures presents a huge challenge in agreeing on which of the widely held beliefs is most important and therefore, how we should be of service to each other. Indeed, the opposite of service to - separation from - has been the rule until today. If we are to believe serving life is man's reason for existing, then there must be some common elements, binding values, or driving principles that mankind can agree on, irrespective of our assorted natures. Of course, anything that claims to bind humankind will have to stand up to constant scrutiny. The premise of this philosophy of purpose is that there are at least two principles of which can be agreed upon by virtually all humankind. The overwhelming majority of the world's population, but not necessarily all governments, industries and extremists, can agree upon something, may be mind boggling, but indeed practical.

The first and foremost principle: every person must have the ability to seek out, enjoy, and maintain their own prosperity. Prosperity, by definition, is to have plenty of what is needed for survival. Therefore, every person must be afforded the opportunity to seek out and be able to retain what they need to survive, specifically all physiological needs such as food, water, and shelter, plus be assured safety and rest, the ability to reproduce, and maintain a habitable environment.

The second principle: every person must have the ability to seek out and maintain their desired life and personal peace without disturbance. Disturbance in this case is defined as interrupting a person's chosen condition, within the confines of not disturbing the greater community.

There will always be dissenters of any and all philosophies. This philosophy of service to our fellow man aims to work from the most basic premise, acceptable to the largest common denominator of mankind, notably, to ensure each person the freedom to seek prosperity and peace. Affording and protecting these rights must be man's highest priority to minimize the effects of the growing separation of humanity. Over time, any group or persons not vested in this foundation of service will be obvious purveyors of separation and of acts against humanity.

As evidenced throughout history, every society that has ever existed - great or small - has deviated from keeping service as man's highest purpose. The leaders of these societies either did not recognize, did not care about, or, blinded by their greed, ego and power pursuits, failed any attempt to serve humanity. This denial has resulted in intensified separation of humanity. Today, man continues to pursue greed and ego driven quests with the belief that the pursuit of unfathomable wealth and unmatched fame will lead to unequaled happiness, but at immeasurable cost to humanity as the gap widens between rich and poor.

Finding Purpose

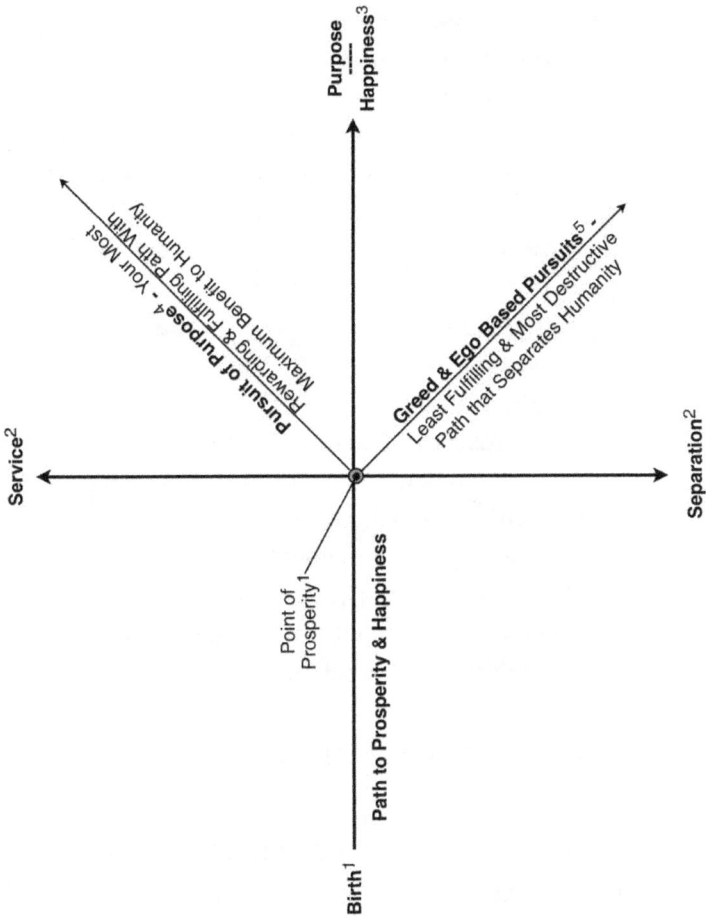

Purpose / Happiness[3]

Service[2]

Separation[2]

Pursuit of Purpose[4] - Your Most Rewarding & Fulfilling Path With Maximum Benefit to Humanity

Greed & Ego Based Pursuits[5] - Least Fulfilling & Most Destructive Path that Separates Humanity

Point of Prosperity[1]

Path to Prosperity & Happiness

Birth[1]

Above: Seeking, Purpose and Happiness: Moving Towards Separation of or Service to Humanity
1. From birth through indoctrination/education/ existence/work to a point of independent prosperity.

Prosperity is the point at which one obtains plenty of what is needed to survive.

2. Service to people and planet (all life forms that contribute to the balance and sustenance of life). Separation of life, losing connection to each other and other forms of life.

3. Purpose and Happiness as goals, after reaching a point of prosperity, are not mutually exclusive in a pursuit of humanitarian purpose but are in greed and ego based pursuits.

4. Pursuit of Purpose ultimate path after reaching a point of prosperity. This path is ripe with ongoing rewards as humanity receives the best of each individual's gifts and contributions.

5. Pursuit of Happiness may be the perceived objective of the individual's greed and ego driven actions. More often it is the acting out of unresolved personal challenges.

Pursuit of Purpose and Happiness

Pursuit of prosperity follows the fulfillment of immediate life giving sustenance. Having met immediate needs, humankind first envisions happiness as having plenty of life's essentials. Today, and more so in earlier times, we need each other's support to grow food, raise a roof, fight fires, assist in birth, and fight wars. The need for assistance binds us to the pack, our community. Our interdependency ensures each other's survival, a shared prosperity, and a level of happiness in our cooperative community. Now, free societies allow us to be more independent with increasingly larger companies providing the bulk of our needs and employment for great numbers of the population.

The United States of America is a good example of a society steeped in meeting the needs of the greater part of its population. America has been the standard bearers of the world with such virtues as guaranteeing all citizens the right to life, liberty, and the pursuit of happiness: a noble declaration and the envy of many peoples. America has also demonstrated, time and again, it's ability to rise to the occasion and to lead on the moral high ground. However, the United States' current state of affairs is demonstrating the United States is in distress with rising exportation of industry, near economic collapse, contaminated food products, political gridlock, religious scandals, mass corruption, overuse of prescription drugs, crisis in education, corporate fraud and wars of uncertain purpose, to name but a few. What has brought the greatest nation in the history of the modern world to this place and predicament?

America's moral fabric appears to be tearing at it's seams while service to humanity gives way to greed and power. While any intelligent examination would be hard pressed to point at one single cause for America's wavering, it would be difficult to not to tie much of it's troubles on pervasive greed and ego based agendas in industry and government. But why?

Pursuit of happiness has no moral code or specific direction. Today, institutions, corporations and politicians are demonstrating how fast the pursuit of happiness, without a moral compass, can unravel without the people's participation. America's Constitution or Declaration of Independence do not inherently hold any pretense that man's purpose in life is to serve humankind, but holds the citizenry responsible for participating in a democratic process thereby ensuring the will of the people is being acted on by government. Many years have passed in America, with a complacent voting populace, at a time when individual and special interests were peeking with greed and ego agendas.

This took time to occur in America and began to show at the end of slavery with the advent of mechanized industry. In this new era of industrialization, self-reliance began to give way to employment by industry, fast growing cities, and corporation's supply of goods and services. The population gradually became more dependent on industry to provide a means of support and government when employment was not available. Personal purpose was reduced to missions of industry and direction of the government. While the masses grabbed hold of industry employment with objectives of becoming prosperous, the established and newly independent grabbed hold of the concept of seeking happiness.

The problem with the worthy pursuit of happiness, without some sort of a ethical guide, is how easily the seeking can degenerate to become one motivated by ego and greed. With the idea that greater prosperity for oneself can bring greater happiness the line that crosses over from prosperity into greed gets blurred. However, a purpose of service has an unmistakable direction with a universal moral high ground. Serving our fellow man does not maintain an open door to greed and ego that requires one to separate themselves from others, from humanity.

For example, most corporations have missions to deliver profits as their highest priority and it becomes the employees purpose to fulfill their mission. Employees, eager to be prosperous and deluded with higher salaries and bigger benefits, then trade personal purpose with the convoluted sense of values their corporate mission has to humanity. When personal purpose is over shadowed by another's mission, careful examination must be given to the mission's alignment with the principles of service to humanity and the possible sacrifice of personal purpose.

Our sense of personal missions and a common purpose for humanity are often compromised with our desire to be prosperous and taking on the missions of others. Such pursuits requires conscious or unconscious belief that we are separate from other people or life, in order to justify our greed or ego motivated behavior. Most of us have and do exhibit such behavior at times, but now growing numbers of individuals, groups and entities are focused on the separation of life as an acceptable means to personal ends. The line between behavior that serves or separates humanity has been blurred for the sake of profits by feeding greed and inflated egos. In order to survive, we will have to consciously reconnect with a sense of personal purpose that is aligned with a common belief that service is our purpose.

Greed, Ego and Separation

The opposite of "service to humanity" is "separation of humanity", as the former bridges the gaps that separate people by recognizing the needs of others (brother's keeper) and the latter in favor of selfish desires (survival of the fittest). Service orientation recognizes that which we have in common and supports humanity. Greed and ego concerns requires one to view oneself as special or separate, to consciously justify their actions (unwillingness to take part in the whole of humanity). While peace and prosperity are the natural outcomes of service, the devices that continuously promote separation are excessive ego and greed.

Regardless of the motivators that promote greed and ego based actions, seeking prosperity puts both service and separation on the same path, which can make it difficult to tell them apart. Because service and separation are on the same path, one can easily be misguided without some manner of discerning between the two. Where does one draw the line? To judge another's prosperity as greed or ego driven is a serious and difficult matter, though one may easily recognize the greed laden missions of some corporations to "maximize shareholder investments." As a result, there is a real need to clearly define greed and ego based behavior so that individuals and communities have some measuring stick to consider their own behavior and make conscious choices in support of humanitarian service versus separation.

For example, you own a food establishment, doing what you love and brings you plenty of what you need. Your customers are happy with the food value and you are prosperous. A sales rep from a food supplier visits you and shows how you can double your income by simply replacing one quality product with one that is less costly, considerably less nutritious, and even potentially dangerous. You've heard the economy could get bad and you are sure no one will notice the change in the product, so you go with the inferior product. Is this market necessity or greed? Where do you draw the line? There is a clear need to understand greed in a measurable manner.

"*Greed* begins at a point after a person's, group's or entity's needs have been met (a state of prosperity) and the product or service being provided to others begins to diminish in value."

Greed is not readily identified by outsiders and can only be accurately judged by the individual,group or the entity, as access to all relevant information has to be considered. Only at the point in which greed and/or egocentric behavior become blatantly obvious can one distinguish a loss of service orientation or vice versa. Understandably, one person's desire can be another's need. Such a conundrum begs the clear distinction of the elements associated with separation of humanity.

"Separation is the division of humanity that allows any person, group, or entity dominance or the ability to negatively impact the condition of another group. Greed and ego based pursuits require separation to justify their interests in diminishing the value of products and services needed by others."

"Ego is noted when it is employed excessively to address a perceived need, in such a way that it negatively impacts the quests of others to seek and maintain their own peace or prosperity."

For example, you own a food establishment, doing what you love and brings you plenty of what you need. Your customers are happy with the food value and you are prosperous. A competitor opens across the street from you, doesn't noticeably affect your business, but brings large crowds, giving you a feeling that you are second best. News media is called to a scene across the street and call on you as a witness to an ambulances appearance there and you take the opportunity to suggest that, "It was probably food poisoning, from what I can tell."

Greed and ego based pursuits lend themselves to separating people, however unintentional, as both deprive another's ability to seek, maintain, or provide products or services. The purposeful reduction in value of a product or service, that meets a need for living, for the reason of added profit of another whose needs are already being met, is out of alignment with man's purpose and is an immoral detestable act. The purposeful taking away of another's right to seek peace and prosperity, in favor of one's egocentric fancy, can be equally offensive.

Using these definitions, consider: If you are indeed serving humanity with personal and collective efforts, in what way is your service measured? How does one determine the value of service? When is your personal purpose not in alignment with service to mankind? When does your personal purpose stop serving and become a disservice to mankind? How do you measure the value of service to mankind provided by entities, like corporations? How are they measured outside of profitability?

Philosophy of Purpose Summarized
Nature is the combination of all living things encompassing man, animals, plants, the environment and all that is required to sustain life. Put another way, all those things required to support life, in all environments of all living things naturally occurring, is nature. We accept that all living things contribute to the balance of nature and the benefit of humanity. Therefore, anything that promotes the separation of humanity is an offense to nature and, therefore, our own humanity.

Finding Purpose

In our effort to evolve as humans, we have sought much that has allowed us unbelievable freedom, from being employed by others to outright separating ourselves from others for self serving reasons, some of which are offensive to humanity. Today, as we have been pushed towards a "market driven" economy, via propaganda, we have also been convinced that much of what we seek is good or in our best interest, but on close examination is abusive to humanity. The lifestyles of some are promoted as models and visions for our own lives, ignoring that we leave others dying, sick, and helpless. Destruction of natural environments and man driven extinction of life is touted as progress. Mankind has inadvertently and/or purposefully become a part of a machine that perpetuates and promotes the separation of nature.

Scientists believe that we are on a path to irreversible destruction of our livable environment in as early as 2050, which puts us in a race to avoid our own extinction. The planet will survive, of course, and perhaps new civilizations will follow. But is it necessary that we go down this path of self-destruction? We need not. We have the power as human beings to right our course and stop the inevitable drive towards extinction. Common and personal is a way, and perhaps the only way.

The path to a lasting humanity is one that recognizes that we are here to serve each other, life, and the environment that life requires. Service to humankind, as man's purpose, is supported by all dominant world religions, is widely accepted in secular circles and supported by science, all together comprising 98% of the world's populace. Service as man's purpose is the foundation that the world's population can build on, promote, and recognize as one thing we have in common. And, in our service to each other, we also recognize that all humans, the stewards of life on earth, demand the two principles in life:

1) the right to prosper - to seek and maintain plenty of what we need,
2) the right to peace - to seek out and maintain our desired living condition without disturbance and within the bounds of our community.

Finding Purpose

Happiness is recognized as a worthy pursuit but without a moral compass there is no reason to support the purpose driven pursuit of service. The paths to happiness and purpose begin on a common path towards prosperity but deviate at the point of reaching individual prosperity. Those oriented to serve, recognize happiness as the resulting benefit or the natural outcome of serving others for the mutual evolution of humankind. Those not on a path of service believe their happiness lies in their fame and fortune, which in effect are greed and ego based desires. In order to justify their desires, they must justify their behavior by separating themselves from others, from humanity.

The point where greed and ego are easily recognized by oneself requires constant and honest self-examination; entities are easily evaluated and open to scrutiny by all. "Survival of the fittest" has become the battle cry of many beyond the point of prosperity, where, "We are our brothers' keeper" is the foundation of service.

Serving each other has been a founding basis of life since the beginning. We must fully embrace this old paradigm to build a new humanity. *Six Steps to Living on Purpose* fully embraces this paradigm with one's personal purpose in life.

This *Philosophy of Purpose* is such a simple and obvious philosophy that children grasp it and comprehend its meaning with ease. Then, why would it be difficult to implement? In a world filled with apathy, loss of hope and divided beliefs that separate us, how can this philosophy ever be implemented to turn our planet into the heaven it could be for all? With wars, disasters, poverty, crime, changing weather and all other distractions we face, how will such a philosophy be launched and embraced? And, what affect will this paradigm have on humanity when we are so deeply divided in consciousness and actions? How do we shift the thinking of others to get on board to allow for a greater shift to occur? The answer is: with you and every other individual taking responsibility for living their lives by pursuing personal purpose.

Finding and following our personal life's purpose is a primary requirement of each of us, that naturally serves humanity. To positively address our pain, follow our passions and use our knowledge, experience and natural talents, benefits everyone. If we are living our purpose, each one of us will be a beacon of inspiration for others and a welcomed leader in whatever we do well. When we step into our purpose, we give others the permission to do the same, we invite and positively challenge others to stand and live a life they want so badly and inspire even more people to do the same. We empower each other to push our boundaries and go where we haven't been before.

Think of the great leaders of this world from Jesus to Martin Luther King, Joan of Arc to Rosa Parks, Gandhi to Mother Teresa, and the numbers of people they individually inspired. Everyone of us is a leader, maybe not in the traditional sense but our words and actions can prove to move those around us. Imagine the exponential growth of each person touching or reaching a few people, or how one person in sincere service to humanity can energize huge populations into action. When we move into our personal purposes, excited with our passions, using our full potential, we can move mountains without wars, without protesting, without loss.

L. Leonard Taylor

"Everybody can be great... because anybody can serve, you don't have to have a college degree to serve. You don't have to make your subject and verb agree to serve. You only need a heart full of grace. A soul generated by love."

~ Martin Luther King Jr.

Part II

Finding Your
Personal Purpose

"I've come to believe that each of us has a personal calling that's as unique as a fingerprint - and that the best way to succeed is to discover what you love and then find a way to offer it to others in the form of service, working hard, and also allowing the energy of the universe to lead you."

~ *Oprah Winfrey*

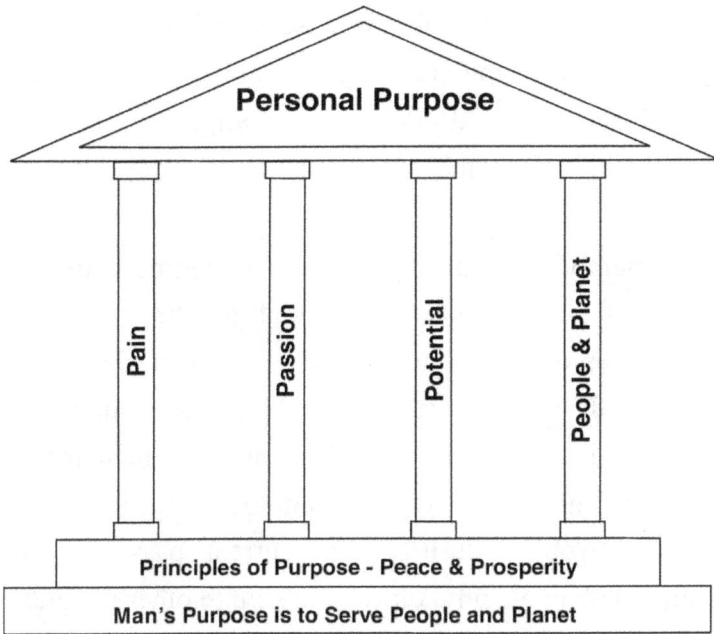

Personal Purpose

Pain | Passion | Potential | People & Planet

Principles of Purpose - Peace & Prosperity

Man's Purpose is to Serve People and Planet

Introduction to the Process of Finding Purpose

Whether you've read the material before this section or not, you can begin the process of identifying personal purpose. The process of finding your personal purpose, your life's purpose, is rather simple and just involves your dedicated time to complete.

The structure of purpose begins with the foundation or mankind's purpose for existing - service to life. The principles of this purpose and the goals of humans are universal - to ensure all are entitled and have rights to seek out and maintain peace and prosperity. By definition personal purpose is aligned with the foundation of humankind's purpose.

This method to finding your purpose begins with four elements of life that are related to the celebrated archetypes of man found in the writings of Carl Jung, Robert Bly and Robert Moore. David Fabricius seizes these concepts in his teachings as key elements to purpose, as well. Your meaningful purpose will consider your enduring pain, current passion, your natural potential and their relationship to other people.

Each of these four areas of our lives are powerful though limited in providing a complete picture of personal purpose on their own. Pain consumes so much of our time that we become experts on this uncomfortable distraction. Passion, often held as our purpose alone, which sometimes changes, can easily take us down a path not in tune with your natural abilities. Potential, our natural, learned skills and experience, can lack motive. While empathy for people may not possess the inspiration to drive a purpose.

During this process, you will brainstorm, shuffle, and define aspects of your life most meaningful to you. You will get naked with yourself, and search out your deepest pains, desires, natural gifts, and empathetic feelings for others. These things become your clues and as you relate the four categories to each other. Your toolbox for living will emerge easily, areas for leadership highlighted, missions of service of which you are well suited become obvious, your gifts to others visibly clear, where you can find your greatest peace and prosperity lay before you. Then, your purpose begins to take shape with meaning that resonates with your life and all will become vividly clear.

The Four Pillars of Purpose

<u>Pain</u>

The pillar of pain is at the heart of personal purpose, as it is usually our central focus and has the greatest impact on our lives. Our minds are consumed with past and possible future events, that are themselves the reasons for our suffering and discomforts. These pains are the result of mental, physical, or emotional trauma that causes us to change our beliefs to protect us from further injury.

Our traumas from childhood, before we developed coping or critical thinking skills, frequently become the stories on which our beliefs are based and have great influence thereafter. Even as adults, unaddressed traumas lead to unwanted beliefs and behaviors. From wherever this pain is derived, it continues to come up at times when we are reminded of the experience. Common trauma from which we suffer include:

- sexual, emotional, and physical abuse
- sustained discrimination
- abject poverty
- terrorism and war
- disasters
- neglect
- medical

We may believe the effects of trauma have been healed, the perpetrators forgiven, and not associate the trailing discomfort and pain with any particular trauma. However, subconscious memory of trauma can be stimulated by visuals, sounds, words and even by a touch, smell or taste. We may be conscious of lasting pain from past trauma, however, left unaddressed, we may not recognize the created beliefs and adapted behavior that have formed.

Our responses to pain or trauma will typically fall into one of three broad categories:

1) negative response: the pain from trauma can result in wildly dangerous beliefs that may lend themselves to feeling separated from others, producing negative and even dangerous behavior;

2) neutral control: aware of pain, we may control our reactions to stimuli although the pain remains;

3) positively addressed: when we positively address our pain, we can move beyond our created beliefs and their auto responses. Addressing pain allows us to heal, change, create new beliefs, help others with similar challenges and be of service to humanity in the elimination of collective pain.

For example, using "sustained discrimination" of African Americans in the USA as an example for each you could find the following results. A negative response to an overwhelming sense of discrimination might result in hatred of those associated with perpetuating the condition, unfairly reacting to all whites in a hostile manner in a perceived discriminatory incident. A neutral response to an overwhelming sense of discrimination, being aware that not all whites discriminate, might be to silently endure the feeling of pain during a perceived discrimination incident. Positively addressing one's pain might be to approach the situation without preconceived ideas of what is taking place, check out the situation properly without attachment and seek justice for all involved.

What are your greatest pains in life? What things seem to trigger undesired behavior for you? Without needing to understand the cause, what ongoing discomforts or pain do you feel in unplanned moments? What causes the pain that has you spend so much time avoiding, contemplating or otherwise focused on, in some way?

If you do not have a major source of recurring pain, discomfort, regrets or hyper sensitivities, ask friends and family or even a mental health professional to be sure you are not suppressing unapproachable pain.

More frequently today, pain, regrets or lasting challenges simply aren't there. The younger you are, the more likely any negative effects of trauma has resulted in lasting pain. Indeed, there are parents and children who have been able to manage or avoid traumatic events without lasting effects. If you are such an individual, you have the promise to epitomize a peaceful existence, effortlessly lead by example and mentor missions of service.

If you are truly pain, discomfort and regret free, then use your deepest empathetic feelings towards the needs of other people or the planet as your healthy approach towards finding purpose. Give in to fervently following your passions and maximizing your potential, which will serve as natural examples to others. What is the source of your most empathetic feelings today? What moves or challenges you regarding the needs and pains of people or planet? What is your greatest empathy for the planet or others?

> *Don't run away from grief, O soul.*
> *Look for the remedy inside the pain,*
> *Because the rose came from the thorn,*
> *And the ruby from the stone.*
>
> *~ Rumi*

Passion

The second pillar of purpose, passion, represents those things that we are just plain psyched out about doing. Passion arouses our enthusiasm, gives us an intense desire to follow or do something. Maybe it's painting, writing, software engineering, swimming, teaching, gardening, cleaning, acting or caring for the challenged. Passion is anything we do that allows time to fly by without realizing, Passion is the willingness to do something without pay when others get paid to do such work. Passion is the element in purpose associated with great fervor, zeal, spirit and abundant energy. Passion supplies the driving energy of our purposes. Passions can change over a lifetime, often after a life changing event. What do you have a great passion for today?

"Passion is energy. Feel the power that comes from focusing on what excites you."

~ Oprah Winfrey

Potential

The third pillar of purpose - potential - is the collection of personal traits, qualities, and natural abilities as recognized by ourselves and others. Natural abilities are often thought of as God given or inherited gifts. They are the attributes that others see in us as natural capabilities to sing, work with numbers, influence people, tell jokes, write, grow plants, critically think, or whatever we might do that stands out as a strength. If we cannot readily identify our natural strengths, we can ask those who knows us well, from parents and friends to teachers and mentors. Gifts can also be those skills we have learned and mastered. Our potential can be taken for granted and therefore not used in ways most beneficial to ourselves or others to advance our purposes in life. What are our natural gifts, skills and abilities?

"All things will be produced in superior quantity and quality, and with greater ease, when each man works at a single occupation, in accordance with his natural gifts, and at the right moment, without meddling with anything else."

~ Plato

People & Planet

The last pillar of purpose - people & planet - is what we bring in service to other people or our life sustaining planet. Ideally, our purpose will be in complete alignment with service to humanity towards peace and prosperity. This pillar of purpose keeps our efforts focused on meeting the needs of all people ensuring all have an opportunity to prosper and have peace.

Secondarily, this pillar of purpose is to predict and measure our progress in serving the needs of life. This is a challenge because it requires self-governance in addition to collective support and feedback. Working as community lifts the entire collective, while reaching our own level of prosperity is required to feel empowered to help another. Our personal pursuits in life can have a negative impact on humanity and only through constant personal consciousness can we monitor the impact we are having on serving life and not separating.

What needs or desires, of <u>people and planet,</u> can we best serve that would also allow us to positively address our <u>pain,</u> that will be energized by our <u>passions</u> and makes use of our full <u>potential</u>? What personal purpose do we believe will make a difference in people and our planet?

The Process of Finding Your Purpose

The pillars of purpose will begin coming to life now as your own specifics are added in the process. The following step by step process is followed with detailed directions and examples. I recommend reading through to the end of the chapter then returning to start and complete the process.

1) Brainstorm and make lists of items, thoughts, ideas, attributes for each pillar (Example on page 53);

2) Combine brainstormed contents, where possible, into common elements under each pillar. You want to end up with one item for pain and people and no more than 2-4 for passions and potential;

3) Pair up and relate each pillar with every other for keys & clues on purpose (see diagram on page 60);

4) Imagine the power of combined keys, clues, and feel your vision of purpose;

5) Write and refine a statement of purpose. Constant review and revision will prove to create a truly representative and believable statement of you;

6) Speak your statement of purpose everyday, several times a day until it is memorized and you own it!

Brainstorming

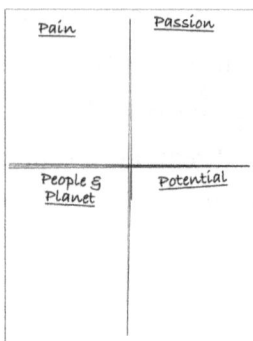

Pain	Passion
People & Planet	Potential

Take a sheet of paper, divide the sheet into four sections by drawing a big plus sign through the middle and then write the name of each pillar as shown. Read the pillar descriptions below, and begin to brainstorm. Alternatively, there are lots of blank pages in the back of the book for your convenience. When you brainstorm, simply write a few words for each thought or idea that comes to mind without judging or thinking about them in the moment. Write these in the corresponding quadrant. Later you will work with these items to pinpoint the most fitting and worthy subjects in each category.

This work is personal and need not be shared with anyone, however, it is important to be honest with yourself. Your pain may be challenging to confront or admit. Your passions could be embarrassing to expose to others. You may think of your potential as meaningless or arrogant in the face of others. What you believe beneficial to people may not appear so useful to you, but there is a place in this world for every gift to meet a real need or desire. Take your time so as not to miss the big or little items, you'll sort them out later. Use the questions below to prompt your brainstorming in each quadrant.

Pain - What hurts when you think about it? What kind of situations, conversations or movies do you avoid? What do you do that negatively impacts your life or the lives of others? What creates fear, discomfort, changes in your moods or behavior? What stops you from doing certain things? What triggers quick changes in behavior? Try to pin down one or more things that come to mind. If you have nothing to list, substitute pain with empathy. What strongly held empathy do you have for others?

Passion - What is something do you just love to do? If you had everything in life you needed, what would you do? What gives you energy, arouses lasting enthusiasm, and allows you to get lost while you are doing it? What would you do for free that others get paid to do today? List at least one passion that qualifies as something you love, would do for free, and you could get lost in doing.

Potential - What are you naturally good at doing? What things do you do better than many or most others? What are you recognized for by others? What have parents, guardians, friends and teachers recognized in you as extraordinary? What skills and abilities have you learned that you are now exceptional at using? List these things as your natural gifts or learned skills and abilities that standout.

People & Planet - When you look at the world and see challenges and needs of people, plants, animals and earth, what do you find to be of great need. What need or desire of others do you feel you would be good at meeting? What cause or challenge do you feel called to contribute time, energy, or money? What cause, challenge, need or desire, do you feel you could be of great assistance? List those things that could make a difference in the lives of others, be they needs or desires.

Combining and Tightening Contents

Now, if at all possible, we want to narrow the contents of this brainstorm down to one cohesive meaningful representation for each category. Here we want to combine items with a common theme and eliminate any items that aren't strongly felt.

Below are the results of my brainstorm as an example:

Pains	Passions
Prejudice & Discrimination	Writing
Social & Nature Injustices	Video & Photography
Heartbreak from Love	Mysteries, History & Truth
Snobbery & Rejection	Inspirational Stories
People & Planet	**Potential**
Opportunity to Prosper	Translating Between Groups
Accountable Leadership	Communicating/ Marketing
Justice & Peace	Organizing & Team Build
How to Get on Track	Creative Problem Solving

The following are example statements created from my above brainstormed list after being combined and tightened.

<u>Pain</u> - There is a common thread between three of the four items listed under the pain pillar with *Heartbreak from Love* being the odd one. I combine *Prejudices & Discrimination, Social & Nature Injustices and Snobbery & Rejection* to become something that resonates with me. The painful feeling of being unfairly judged, discriminated against or rejected boils down to feeling separated from others, which appears to be a common theme. Experiencing any one of these three items results in that same painful feeling. However, the *Heartbreak from Love* and stands alone from the other theme.

In comparison, the heartbreak is not nearly as strong and definitely secondary in the big scheme of pain. Because of the strong feelings in the one area of life, I will focus my attention on the three dominant indicators of pain I experience. I am not letting go of this secondary source of pain, it too needs to be dealt with but one pain at a time for now. Summarizing this life affecting pain, I've come to this statement: *My pain is feeling less than others and believing that I am not as significant to mankind, as others.*

Take your time with the items identified as painful and combine those that are similar, eliminate those that are not truly critical or are secondary in nature. Find a common theme if more than one item remains. Write a simple statement of your pain. If you have no pain, then write a statement of your most empathetic feeling of the pain of other people or the planet.

Passion - I have a lot of passions, this could be tricky. However, when I begin considering what I like about each of these items, I realize there is a common theme. In general and common to all passions here, are stories - creating stories via writing, video & photography as much as reading, listening to and watching stories. Knowledge of self quickly gives me that understanding, without any doubt. I may not consciously know how these things will play solidly into my purpose, at this point but *My passion is storytelling.*

Passions are not whims or things you might like, so first eliminate those items of which you are not certain. If you have more than one item remaining, find the common theme. If you have no passions, identify one thing you would really like to try, sample, or give a chance. Write a simple statement for your passion.

Potential - These items don't appear very related in any way but when I stop to consider what could be done with these skills and abilities, I can envision alignment with man's greater purpose to serve each other. I can see a bigger picture of bringing people together, solving problems between them, organizing using my communications and marketing skills to find common ground. Wow, this is something I would not have considered. I might want someone objective, who knows me, to tell me what they think of this. On the other hand, my heart is beating as if I know I am being called to do something now. *My potential, natural and learned gifts, is in bringing people and projects together for execution.*

Potential are gifts that you possess, that you may or may not use. If you are not using these gifts, ask yourself if they are truly gifts and eliminate those that are not exceptional and look for a common connection between the remaining gifts. Write a simple statement of your natural and learned skills and abilities.

People & Planet - Reviewing my brainstorm of what people and planet need, and narrowing it down to one cohesive statement: that the *Opportunity to Prosper* is like an umbrella over *Accountable Leadership, Justice and Peace* and *How to Get On Track*. There three items are all required or are part of having more *Opportunity to Prosper*. The main theme here, *Opportunity to Prosper* also aligns with the foundation and principles of *service as our purpose*. "Justice" and "Peace", I think, are not necessarily connected, as peace is very much individually defined. Pursuing peace will be covered more in the next section, for now I will remove it from my list. This is getting interesting, assuming I am headed in the right direction. I think this statement is in tune with my feelings of the needs of people and planet: *My people and my planet need more opportunity to prosper.*

People and our planet need more solutions than any individual has answers. So, if you have multiple unconnected items, do away with those you don't feel you could dedicate an effort towards. Find the common theme with the remaining items, if more than one. What remains should be a need or desire of people or the planet that a product or service can meet. Can you see yourself getting behind such a product or service? If so, write a statement reflecting your belief in what people or the planet needs or desires without being specific about service or product. If not, either broaden your view of or reconsider what you feel people need. Write a statement.

Completing this exercise has probably aroused your enthusiasm for finding purpose and given you some insights. You may have started relating these elements to each other looking for that whole purpose, no? When relating these areas to each other, give consideration to how you manage these four key elements in your life today. More specifically, how does your positive or negative treatment of your pain affect your purpose. What happens if you don't follow your passion or you minimize your potential or not cater to the needs of others? Before you draw any conclusions, let's look at the positive and negative of each pair of pillars.

Pairing the Pillars for Perspectives on Purpose
Every pillar (white center boxes) can be matched with every other to provide valuable information about our

purpose. In the table below, we can find a range of possibilities that have extreme positive (light gray) and negative (darker gray) possible outcomes, depending on how we address or ignore these elements. Consider the six possible pillar pairs made horizontally, vertically and diagonally on the chart, to find the beneficial attributes as well as their possible distraction from our most meaningful purpose.

Leadership Opportunities	Service Missions	Personal Tools	Inspires People
Ego Based Pursuits	Pain	Passion	Path to Peace
Greed Based Pursuits	People	Potential	Path to Prosperity
Limits Growth	Perpetuates Problems	Limits Authenticity	Deters Leadership

■ Unconscious/Misdirected Approach ☐ Conscious/Purposeful Approach

Above Diagram: Keys and Clues of Combined Pairs

<u>Pain & Passion</u> have one really big thing in common - if they are not both being addressed productively, they will occupy a lot of time, thinking time. Without positively addressing pain, reminders of your pain will constantly pop up in daily life. The bad feelings and inappropriate reactions, stimulated by all kinds of outside influences, will cause dysfunction in a way that interrupts freedom of thought in the present. If not chasing passions, the mind will constantly expend energy thinking of getting back to that which is craved so much. You've heard it in others: the nagging fear in life or the book they want to write just will not let them have any peace. Yes, *peace*. These two pillars, pain & passion, are connected because they are directly related to attaining any measure of peace.

Addressing pain and chasing passions allows greater mind activity in the present, opening the door to living on purpose, the focus of this book. When pains are effectively dealt with, less conscious effort is spent judging the past. Passions, when not pursued will typically keep the mind focused on the future with worry about those things that can keep us from doing what we want.

Addressing pains and passions means to pursue the challenges associated with being stuck and prevents us to living our lives fully. Addressing our pains directly - identifying sources, reactions and beliefs - allows us to create new beliefs which will remove the obstacles of falsely held beliefs and judgements about ourselves. When working fully with passions, high energetic states are reached, the brain finds a desired healthy zone - homeostasis. Freed of pain and immersed in passion is a blissful state of mind, it is peace.

The two common approaches to pain and passion are ignoring and letting go. Both suggest pain and passion no longer exists or are successfully subdued. However, "letting go", often the goal in spiritual practice, counseling, and transformational techniques, is a commitment to working through the challenge of pain and finding the resistance that stops you from chasing your passions.

Attempts to "ignore" the regular stimulations that activate pain and passion are tantamount to believing that the fast moving train coming towards you, will not hurt you. In both cases, unaddressed pain and passion will eventually show up in some undesired fashion and limit your ability to manifest personal greatness in the present. (Greatness is the recognized element in you that is most worthy of consideration by, and benefit to, others.) Finding peace is best pursued off the tracks of fast moving trains.

Equally important, if you are actively challenged with pain and distracted from attending passions, the prospects of negatively affecting people and planet becomes a very real possibility. Delusional and egocentric actions are common responses to unaddressed pains and passions. A repetitive example of an extreme negative outcome, is witnessed every so often in our media as mass gun shootings. In every one of these cases, it is found that the perpetrators felt like outcasts or separated from the greater society. Their pain, as found by psychologists, was so great and unattended, they developed a passion to get revenge.

We are obligated in principle, as a society, to ensure every person has access to pursue plenty of what they need for survival, to meet individual need and to avoid sending anyone to such a distraught point. We can prevent such disasters from occurring by giving focus to our pain and following our passions. Looking back at my example:

My pain of feeling less than others, and believing that I am not as significant to mankind, can be positively addressed in conjunction with my passion for story-telling. I can use my desire to tell stories to review those occurrences in my life which may give me insights as to why I am not doing all that I can today. I could also work with a counselor for direction, get involved in some transformational activities and spend more time being meditative, all proven methods of relieving pain and moving into passions.

In dealing with my challenge and following passions in this way, I can make progress, feel better about where I am in this world and avoid harmful ego based pursuits. More importantly, if I am approaching pain and passion head on, I will find a higher level of peace.

What ideas come to mind when considering how to directly address pain and follow passion?

<u>People & Potential</u> connects the needs of people with one's natural talents, which ideally results in both personal prosperity and value to humanity. On the other end of the spectrum, the same pair can lead to greed when not in alignment with man's purpose to serve. In my example, potential - natural and learned gifts - is in bringing people and projects together for execution to meet people and planet needs for more opportunity to prosper, could turn to greed by simply using skills to take advantage of people's needs. As an example, I could use marketing skills to sell get rich quick schemes to fleece the needy and enhance my wealth, a common offering in a society bent on excessive greed.

In a more positive approach to my talents and peoples need, would be in working with members of my community to organize around a project for mutual benefit. My particular desire would be around creating more "opportunity to prosper" from farmers' markets to community based information to assist those who lack resources to gain the assistance needed to grow.

How can you use your inherent skills and abilities to meet your needs and those of others?

Finding Purpose

<u>People & Pain</u>, when combined, reveal the basis for personal missions of service. With an understanding of one's own pain, working with those experiencing the same or similar pain could lead to mass healing and massive steps in human evolution. Imagine the amplified effect of many addressing their pain and using it to serve others with the same problem.

Not recognizing the need to both positively address pain and serve the needs of others would perpetuate the pain and continue to separate people. For example, imagine a like-minded group suffering the same kind of misery from military drone strikes, might come together to promote damaging perceptions and end up forming a terrorist group, fomenting separation of people.

My positive example would be recognizing my pain of being discriminated against, as found in most groups of people, is an opportunity to serve others by helping them to identify, positively deal with by recognizing the false perceptions and eliminating made up stories and inherited beliefs. I can also help those unaware of this suffering, to become more sympathetic and sensitive to promote healing.

How could you positively address your torment and help others with similar feelings?

Potential & Passion represent the tools, mediums and methods that move one's purpose. The energy inherent in working with passions coupled with the potential of natural gifts combine as a powerhouse of efficient activity. Used affirmatively, expertise is unrestrained and available. Used negatively, these same elements will stifle great innovation, waste evolutionary growth, and can be used as tools to separate humanity.

My marketing skills and my passion for storytelling are tools capable of influencing people.

What tools, mediums & methods are available to you and how could they be used to serve you and humanity?

Potential & Pain pillars represents unique leadership opportunities when approached positively and utilized for the benefit of others. Such opportunities are lost when pain is left to fester or personal potential is used without consideration of impact to mankind.

Finding Purpose

Considering my skill set, I will demonstrate leadership by openly addressing my long endured pain by specifically communicating and seeking solutions wherever the opportunity presents itself.

How can you use your gifts to lead others in dealing with similar pain or your most empathetic feelings?

<u>People & Passions</u> come together as powerful inspiration for others, when properly delivered from the heart with passion. Expressed passion brings contagious enthusiasm, inspiring others to higher levels of conscious effort in any area of life. When we do not embrace our passions, they will lack luster to inspire and may even have the opposite affect on others. Overly egocentric driven passions may deter others from pursuing their own common passions out of fear they too may appear as egomaniacs.

My meaningful and passionately told stories of interest, told to those who can relate, could easily energize and inspire some beyond their current limits and into their own purpose.

How could your positive treatment of people & passions help meet your needs and humanity's?

Now, if you haven't, relate your four pillars of purpose in pairs to find more clues into your own purpose. Starting horizontally, how do your pains relate to your passions in finding personal *peace*? How can your potential skills meet needs of people and create your *prosperity*? Go through all six pairs to find big clues for your life's purpose.

Using Keys & Clues to Find Your Vision

Keys to your purpose consist of your four summarized statements from the brainstorm. Clues are from the pairing of pillars you just finished. By simply having all of this information in front of you, you should be able to begin to see a bigger picture of how these things come together. Here is the all-encompassing four part question that you will need to summarize your purpose:

How can you positively address your pain, fervently follow passions using your natural and learned skills to meet needs and desires of people while having a positive impact on humanity?

Finding Purpose

From my example, my keys are:
- Separated - less than others, not good enough
- Storytelling - speaking, writing, showing
- Team Builder - organizing, marketing, problem solving, communicating
- Need Opportunity - leadership, justice, direction

My clues are:
- Write stories about pain to understand and heal
- Organize & team building for meaningful projects
- Positively addressing common pain in groups
- Storytelling & marketing to make a difference
- Standing up, being open with every opportunity
- Tell meaningful stories to inspire & energize others

My feelings are:
- I want to eliminate the feeling of being separated from humanity for all, by;
- telling meaningful stories that inspire others to stand up and live purposely;
- bring together those prepared to create community projects to benefit all;
- offering greater opportunity to find peace and prosperity.

Play with your keys and clues. What's coming up for you? What are your feelings towards these revelations that you've always really known?

Writing Your Statement of Purpose

Feel your way into your purpose statement and keeping all aspects included, it should flow naturally. Remember, pain is at the heart of your purpose, but all pillars are being attended to here. You can break your statement into more than one sentence, if needed, or allow it to be a run on. What is important is that you feel it, own it, that it is a part of your authentic self.

You want your statement of purpose to be action and solution oriented but broad enough that you don't have to change it every time you take on a new mission. For example, I know I prefer to be project oriented, so rather than stating that my purpose is to "fight racial discrimination" I might use, "build bridges over the gaps that separate individuals and groups," keeping it action and solution oriented but broad enough so that I take up any form of separation. This purpose absorbs my specific pain and is broad enough to take on the pain of the handicap, ethnic or religious groups.

Next, my passion is all about "storytelling" so how about "I handle my purpose by telling meaningful and inspiring stories." My potential is zeroed in on "team building." Lastly I want to include people's needs. So, I have come up with this initial statement:

My purpose in life is to build bridges over those gaps that separate individuals and groups, to tell stories, build teams and meet needs.

Okay, that's a pretty dry statement. I want my purpose to be meaningful, inspiring, and arousing. I want more description and power in my statement. Maybe this:

My purpose in life is to build bridges over the gaps that separate people. I do this by facing my pain positively, telling powerful stories that inspire, maximizing my natural skills of organizing, marketing, team building and problem solving, to meet needs of people to have greater opportunity for peace and prosperity.

Write your statement of purpose, sit with it, rewrite it, sleep on it, and improve it. Read it aloud until it rolls off your tongue as smoothly as you wrote it. Embrace your final version of your purpose.

Knowing and Using Your Statement of Purpose

Your purpose in life represents you, it is your calling card, it stands when you are sleeping, your guiding light when you are awake and a beacon for those looking for your gifts. You created this purpose from a deep inner knowing of yourself, now emblazon it into your memory. State it and write it, first thing every morning until it is solidly memorized. Speak it every chance you get. State it at the beginning of any address. Recite it when someone asks you about yourself. Soon, if not immediately, you will find yourself standing taller, worthy of the purpose of your life. Your known purpose will keep you focused and serve to inspire others to live more purposeful lives.

In order to fully live a life of purpose, in alignment with man's principles or purpose, you will need to *positively address your pain, fervently follow your passion and maximize your potential to meet needs of people, while monitoring the impact your actions have on humanity.*

Your purpose will continue to change and mature as you live and experience new avenues in your life. Remain open to modify it as needed. Purposes do change in life and the younger you are, the more likely it will change as you learn more about yourself. That is not to say that you can't identify a purpose but to be open to change.

Use the space below and the back of book to write your statement of purpose till it feels good meets your need.

_____

_____

_____

_____

_____

_____

_____

_____

_____

_____

_____

_____

_____

_____

_____

_____

_____

_____.

Summarizing Purpose

Living with purpose is an old concept, it is what we had to do without thinking. When we consciously identify and pursue a personal purpose in life we avoid being distracted and defaulting into an unconscious purpose. There were times when technology was not as prevalent, corporations not as dominant, and human beings worked with a great deal more conscious purpose. Ask a survivor of the depression or World War II years and you'll get a better sense of purposeful lives. Living with purpose has now become a necessity for all humankind as we approach climatical points of no return, energy challenges, food supply concerns along with a renewed sense of responsibility and justice for all of earth's inhabitants.

Survival of the human species is everyone's concern and responsibility. Leaving the hugely politicized challenges of today in the hands of governments or anyone else to resolve, may ultimately prove irresponsible on our part.

"Everyone has a purpose in life... a unique gift or special talent to give to others. And when we blend this unique talent with service to others, we experience the ecstasy and exultation of our own spirit, which is the ultimate goal of all goals."

~ Deepak Chopra

References

Taylor, Lawrence Leonard. *Six Steps to Living on Purpose*. Lahaina: New World Publishing and Promotions, 2014. Electronic and Print Books.

The World Factbook 2013-14. Washington, DC: Central Intelligence Agency, 2013.

Isaiah 43.7. The Holy Bible.

Diamond, Jared. *Collapse: How Societies Choose to Fail or Succeed. New York: Penguin Group, 2005. Print.*

Kenny, Charles. *Americans! Stop Worrying and Learn to Love Decline: Why 2014 will be our best year yet.* Internet: POLITICO, January 07, 2014. Electronic. www.politico.com/magazine/story/2014/01/decline-is-good-for-america-101749.html#ixzz30bibCxcX

UC Santa Barbara. Retrieved 2012-11-09. Voter Turnout in Presidential Elections: 1828 - 2008. The American Presidency Project.

Ollman, Bertell. *Market Economy: Advantages and Disadvantages.* Talk at Nanjing Normal University, Nanjing, China. October 1999

von Radowitz, John. Climate change timeline is shocking - scientists. TimesofMatla.com. Electronic. www.timesofmalta.com/articles/view/20131011/environment/Climate-change-timeline-is-shocking-scientists.489854. October 11, 2013.

References

Fabricius, David W.A. Vital Seven. Internet webinar. August 2013.

ManKind Project. New Warrior Training Adventure. Hawaii. Therapeutic event. September 2013

Moore, Robert. *King, Warrior, Magician, Lover: Rediscovering the Archetypes of the Mature Masculine.* New York: HarperCollins, 1990. Print.

Jung, Carl G. *The Archetypes and The Collective Unconscious (Collected Works of C.G. Jung Vol.9 Part 1).* New York: Princeton Press, 1969. Print.

Scaer, Robert. *The Trauma Spectrum: Hidden Wounds and Human Resiliency.* New York: W.W. Norton & Company, 2005. Print.

Rumi. Streep, Meryl. Hamid, Moshin. Winfrey, Oprah. Plato. Gandhi, Mahatma. Brainy Quote: Internet. www.brainyquote.com, 2001-2014. Electronic.

Wilson, Edward Osborne. *Evolution and Purpose of Man*, interview. Arlington: Public Broadcasting Corporation. Charlie Rose Program. April 5, 2014. Television.

Winfrey, Oprah. Patanjali. Chopra, Deepak. Einstein, Albert. Trans4Mind, Ltd. Quotes. www.trans4mind.com Internet. 1997-2014.

An Introduction to

Six Steps to
LIVING ON
PURPOSE

By L. Leonard Taylor

SIX STEPS TO

Living

ON

PURPOSE

TRANSFORMING YOUR
PAIN, PASSION & POTENTIAL
INTO
PEACE, PROMISE & PROSPERITY

L. LEONARD TAYLOR

"Our deepest fear is not that we are inadequate. Our deepest fear is that we are powerful beyond measure. It is our light, not our darkness that most frightens us. We ask ourselves, Who am I to be brilliant, gorgeous, talented, fabulous? Actually, who are you not to be? You are a child of God. Your playing small does not serve the world. There is nothing enlightened about shrinking so that other people won't feel insecure around you. We are all meant to shine, as children do. We were born to make manifest the glory of God that is within us. It's not just in some of us; it's in everyone. And as we let our own light shine, we unconsciously give other people permission to do the same. As we are liberated from our own fear, our presence automatically liberates others."

~ Marianne Williamson

TABLE OF CONTENTS

Preface

We go through life changing from moment to moment and, over time, become different people according to our environmental conditioning, beliefs and desires. We also change as a result of traumatic and significant events like losing someone close, end of a long term relationship or our own near death experience. Change, by chance, happens whether we like it or not. But what about the times when we consciously want a change? What do we do when we want to rid ourselves of bad habits, dump our frustrating lives or just want out of impossible situations? What if we want to embrace something new, accomplish something different, be something we have never been or have something we have never had?

At some point in our lives, most of us want to change, transform our lives or go beyond previous accomplishments. Obstacles are always in the way or appear as overwhelming challenges. Professionals in the fields of human development have studied endlessly on improving or changing the psychological make up of individuals so we can perform better or differently. From prison to military boot camp, group transformation has been made with success but individual change on demand has proven to be a far greater challenge.

We know that change on demand has been difficult not only because we have been short on knowledge and tools but often we were misdirected, short on commitment and lacked the passion that would move us forward in a new quest. We like our comfort zones and moving outside of them requires strength of purpose, which comes with real hunger and a strong belief in our direction. Without real conviction, we waddle in self created ruts, do the same things over, and over hoping something will magically deliver us different results.

We know that revamping our lives is possible. History has documented the greatest people known to man, and today we witness the living great ones in the media. We've heard all kinds of inspirational stories of people overcoming terrible odds to become outstanding individuals doing wondrous things. We owe to ourselves and those who have come before us, to be all that we can be and to inspire those who follow us. And, one day we will come to realize that everyone has seeds of greatness and we are all responsible for watering those seeds so that world bears the fruit we all desire!

May the world benefit from you stepping into your transformation.

L. Leonard Taylor

Introduction

I hated my life. My second marriage was ending, my beloved children were with their mothers. I had fallen from grace on my job—I was demoted and demoralized. My income was half of my expenses, I rented my car to a coworker because I could not afford the car payment. I lacked any real friends and my social skills were limited. I was an understated introvert afraid of my own shadow. Yes, I was a shadow of a man. I was financially, emotionally and spiritually bankrupt. At 33 years of age, I was a broken man with a broken life, and I hated it.

Yet somehow I knew I had something greater in me, I knew I had something worthy to give the world. I knew I was better than what I was giving and getting from my less than mediocre life. All around me was the same uninspired life. I wanted more, so much more, but had no clue how to find life beyond my day to day existence, doing the same things over and over. Getting off this merry-go-round seemed impossible.

I made a desperate attempt to find some direction with one of the last purchases of my soon to be cancelled credit card. From a mail order catalogue, I found an audio program - Seeds of Greatness by Dennis Waitley. I knew nothing about this man but the promotion suggested that with this program there was a chance to find a better life. What did I have to lose? Weeks later, the package arrived and I became obsessed with Dr. Waitley's take on life and belief in how much human's can achieve.

Dr. Waitley represented a new beginning. He was offering a ticket on a train I had never traveled. I listened to his words, so many words, of hope and encouragement and did not hesitate to get onboard. This train started moving, with my desire for a better life and to be a better man, I could envision clear rails ahead of me. I began gleaning practical information from my new friend, and the first two steps toward change became very clear.

I surrounded myself with inspirational speakers, agents of change and leaders with new messages of hope. I began soaking in their positive messages, that filled me with unlimited possibilities for a better life. Their messages led me to setting goals for the first time in my life, moving me to re-educate myself and study subjects that would eventually help me find the life I never had but always imagined. I delved into subjects that helped me understand how I had come to my beliefs and other subjects that challenged what I had accepted as truths about myself and my world.

My obsession to change drew me to subjects like mind control, self hypnosis, subconscious programming, subliminal messaging, therapeutic music, all of which I crafted into useful tools and methods to usher in my own transformation. Slowly, without realizing, I began formulating a process that would alter my life forever. From the gifts of so many others, I created this handbook—a tailored process for change. This book summarizes, in a simple step by step process, how to create and implement a personal program for real and significant change.

"In Order to Have Something You've Never Had or Be Something You've Never Been, You'll Have to Do Something You've Never Done!"

~ *L. Leonard Taylor*

The Process for Effective Change

This process for effective change is not rocket science though every step of this process has brain and mind science at its core. The simple steps here have been derived from numerous sources and combined to create a program requiring minimal time, painless effort and little money. Aspects of this process could be viewed as techniques used in brainwashing. "Brainwashing" is most often associated with secret cults, murderous madmen or even government programming while the word itself, could be compared with something as useful as bathing, doing laundry or washing a car. Considering the negative connotations "brainwashing" conjures up for us, lets have refer to this part of the process as it is "brain cleansing."

I believe it is our responsibility to cleanse our brains regularly, for the same reason we clean anything. We absolutely need to flush out the uselessly old, habitually bad and the fictitiously false thoughts and beliefs we pick up on our way to wherever we are headed. There is no wonder why we too often continue down the same path hoping for different results—we never seem to voluntarily clean our brains with updated directions.

With this brain cleanse, we can expect our our path to be clear, our focus to be sharpened and our purpose always in the forefront. A good brain cleanse is the simple, very effective and direct method to change the oil, tune up the car, check the tires and wash the car in preparation for a road trip.

However, and more accurately, this process for change involves more than brain-cleansing. It involves the reprogramming and protection of your newly created direction. When followed, you will end up with a program that will take you where you decide to go. Of course, your destination is a choice, so, there must be clarity as to where you are going, who you will be and what you will do. For this reason, a chapter has been included on *How to Find Your Purpose* though the intent of this book is not to define your purpose but to put you on a path of *living* your purpose.

The mission of this book is to offer a process that can be customized individually, to make a major change in your life. There is no real mystery to this process, the power is in the combined use of the individual steps. The individual steps in this book are not new but have been the subject of study by scholars and science, contemplated by spiritual masters, tested and documented. The six simple steps are plainly identified as:

1) **Stop** or minimize the negative influences in life (can't see the forest when surrounded by trees.)

2) **Start** adding attitude altering content to daily life (choose mind food wisely, we are what we eat!)

3) **Assess** current position in this world today (need to know where you are to plot a destination!)

4) **Plan** life with goals & milestones with a roadmap (driving cross country is easier with a map!)

5) **Program** the conscious & subconscious with same plan (make right & left hands work together!)

6) **Affirm** desires, cement beliefs and reject the negative (remember to go towards the light).

Individually, these steps are simple to implement. Together, these steps are powerful life changing tools giving back personal responsibility, defining direction and exercising the greatest amount of control over individual peace and prosperity. This is a simple step by step "how to" book, using real tools that will result in significant change. These six steps will deliver transformation to those seeking major change.

"How long? How long will this take?", is the most frequently asked question. The truthful answer is, the commitment and effort given to the program is directly related to the time required to make a change. If television, as your regular sensory input and whose content is discontinued or replaced with a diet of positive material, noticeable changes will be observed quickly. An honest assessment and the creation of a solid plan with goals, will produce immediate progress. However, a part-time 'off and on' effort could result in failure altogether. Unfortunately, it would be irresponsible to quote the time required in this process for making *your* personal effective change, as it is directly related to your dedication and desire.

For nine months, I spent hours researching, experimenting, planning and programming, which resulted in success never imagined. Unlike my unplanned approach of identifying programs and building processes, you have the opportunity to immerse yourself from the start. There is no need take months studying and building a program. You can immediately jump into these six steps and note changes in days and radical transformation in weeks; you are the beneficiary of my exercise and success. I believe you will implement change at a much faster rate. However, caution should be used not to fall into the western expectation of *instant gratification*, discouragement may be the reward.

These steps are simple, but passion and commitment play a significant role in changing long held beliefs, old habits and years of reinforcing programming. Dedicate yourself to this process and create the desirable change in your life, painlessly and quickly.

These tools and instructions will lead you through custom designing a program to put you on a track to meet your most ambitious desires. In a simple step by broken down step, you will learn how to create the change you want in your life.

May your metamorphosis begin now, so that you live the life you desire and your transformation benefits all humanity.

L. Leonard Taylor

"The Mind is Much Like a Computer –
Garbage In, Garbage Out!"
~ Modern American Proverb

Step One:
Stop the Negative Influences in Your Life

Researchers and media experts report that we are bombarded with thousands of negative messages daily. In the first step of this program, we will minimize most of these messages from our mainstream media. Adherence to this simple step will significantly impact how fast change can occur. Our mainstream media is filled with negative messages, subliminal messaging and time killing content, all of which are distractions to reaching any destination. With the many things we desire in our lives, we must wrestle away our time from external sources to better direct our attention and energy.

More people complain today about their inability to stay focused on a given task. Most of us have experienced starting a task and a few minutes later find ourselves working on something entirely different. What is at the core of this attention deficit disorder? Well, it is possible that this familiar re-prioritizing of tasks is due to the clutter of an overloaded mind. Today, we are overburdened with tasks and incoming information, in the workplace and at home, which is enough to easily drive us away from our intent to the point of distraction.

You can begin gaining greater control of your life by exercising your power over external influences. Only you can fully manage the distraction from television, the Internet, radio, music, newspapers, magazines and other media. Uncontrollable audio, visuals and other sources of influence, will be the focus in step six. For now, we will simply eliminate the potential influence of controllable mainstream sources.

End of Introduction to
Six Steps to
LIVING ON
PURPOSE

You may have a copy sent today from
www.SixStepsToLivingOnPurpose.com

The following pages are for
your personal notes.

Personal Processing Notes

Personal Processing Notes

Personal Processing Notes

Personal Processing Notes

Personal Processing Notes

Personal Processing Notes

Personal Processing Notes

Personal Processing Notes

Personal Processing Notes

Personal Processing Notes

Personal Processing Notes

Author, Lawrence Leonard Taylor

Lawrence Leonard Taylor was exposed to travel by his parents, who were both school teachers that spent free summers towing him and his siblings around the country. Lawrence, as he is better known, left Detroit in the late 70's in search of an identity beyond his city borders. In the U.S. Navy, he became an avid chronicler of his travels to foreign lands in letters to family and friends which drew just enough praise to inspire him to develop his storytelling skills.

Lawrence's first major transformation propelled him, with a growing family, into a career of telecommunications and marketing. In 2005, five years after moving to Hawaii, he began recreating his earlier self-styled transformation. In his recounting of his process he was able to identify six definite steps in his effective change method. Later, he recognized the need for accessing his inner most desires from life long pain, passion, inherent gifts and knowledge and how they could serve others.

Today, Lawrence is a dedicated student of human transformation and a proponent of, finding and living on, purpose. "For me, finding and living with purpose is the personal transformation we all strive to make. When we take back our lives, we make a change, the world opens to us, we connect and co-create to move beyond old beliefs and limitations. The old paradigm of taking what we can becomes giving whatever we can - serving others is more natural than taking, hoarding and senseless greed."

Lawrence is a father and grandfather, loves to hike, swim and travel for exposure and constant change. Lawrence is captivated with the seemingly rapid transformation of people, here and now, and has a passion for developing individual's self sustaining business. Lawrence believes love, exposure and an open mind are best values to personal development. Lawrence's declared purpose in life "is to build broad bridges over the gaps that separate people," and feels certain that "anything that separates people, is not in the best interest of our humanity."

Find more about the author or order books at:
sixstepstolivingonpurpose.com
popular book etailers
barnesandnoble.com
smashwords.com
amazon.com
itunes.com

Other available titles from the author include:
Six Steps to Transformation
Six Steps to Living On Purpose

Acknowledgements

This book would have not been possible without the contributions of many supporters. My parents, Charles and LeClaire Taylor, have been lasting examples of purposeful living while allowing me great breadth in finding purpose. Russian psychologist and best-selling author, Julia Gippenreiter, graciously gifted valuable advice on writing with vulnerability. Contributing editors and friends: Noreen Hamilton, Marie Janowiak, Jeff Heisel and Albert Meyer, seasoned professionals yet gentle with their critiques. Tireless design and marketing support from Andrea Scholz. The Writers Group of Ma'alaea - Mike O'Brien, Eileen Woods, Anjalie Trice, Lois Janice and Bill Meyer, faithfully met weekly to read, review and support each other's writing at: Saltimbocca, the restaurant that served us so graciously. Mr. Bill Comer and my brothers of the ManKind Project that authentically supported me while I sorted aspects of myself and found greater purpose in my life. It is my honor to acknowledge and thank all for the hand up.

www.ingramcontent.com/pod-product-compliance
Lightning Source LLC
Chambersburg PA
CBHW020505030426
42337CB00011B/244